MR. MEN
So Greedy

Roger Hargreaves

In these stories you will meet:

Mr Greedy   Mr Topsy-Turvy

Mr Uppity

And this more difficult word:

house

EGMONT

EGMONT
We bring stories to life

Book Band: Red

MR. MEN   **LITTLE MISS**

MR. MEN™ LITTLE MISS™ © THOIP (a SANRIO company)

So Greedy © 2016 THOIP (a SANRIO company)
Printed and published under licence from Price Stern Sloan, Inc., Los Angeles.
Published in Great Britain by Egmont UK Limited
The Yellow Building, 1 Nicholas Road, London, W11 4AN

ISBN 978 1 4052 8267 3
63468/1
Printed in Singapore

Illustrated by Adam Hargreaves
Series and book banding consultant: Nikki Gamble

Written by Jane Riordan
Designed by Cassie Benjamin

MIX
Paper
FSC   FSC® C018306

So Greedy

This is Mr Greedy.

Hello, Mr Greedy.

Mr Greedy is greedy.

Mr Greedy is big.

Mr Greedy is too big.

Too big for the car.

Too big for the bus.

Mr Greedy was sad.
He went to see
Mr Uppity.

Mr Uppity had too
much in his bags.

Mr Greedy sat on the bags. Mr Greedy shut the bags.

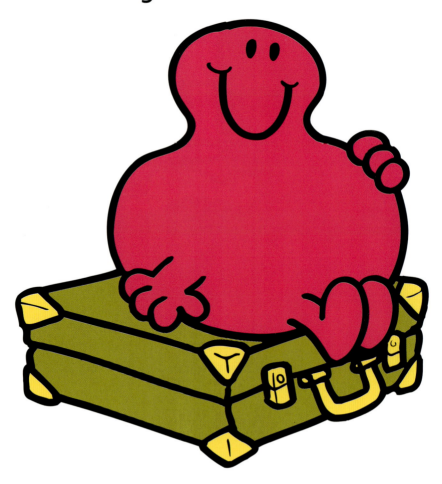

Mr Greedy was happy
to help. Goodbye,
Mr Greedy!

The Round Way Wrong

This is Mr Topsy-Turvy.

Hello, Mr Topsy-Turvy.

Mr Topsy-Turvy is
turvy-topsy ... no ...
topsy-turvy!

He is topsy-turvy in the car.

He is topsy-turvy
on the bus.

Mr Topsy-Turvy
went to find a
topsy-turvy house.

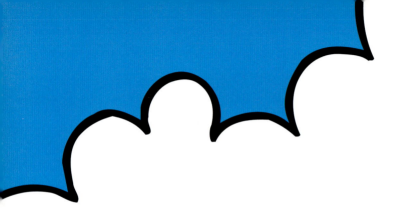

This house?
No, not this house.

This house or
that house?
No, not this
house or that house.

Look at this house!

This house is
topsy-turvy.
This is the house
for Mr Topsy-Turvy.

Goodbye,
Mr Topsy-Turvy.

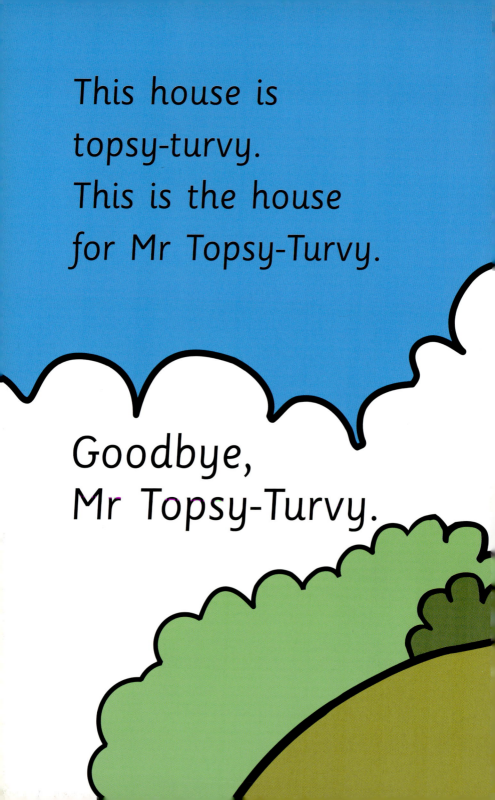

45

Topsy-Turvy Time

Follow the twisty paths to match Mr Topsy-Turvy with the words beginning with a 't' sound. Read the words as you reach them.

tent

train

tree

A Light Lunch

Mr Greedy is having a bite to eat.
Can you read these words and find
them in the tasty picture?

bib   jelly

        cake

                              egg